ELIZABETH CAT

To Barbara Sawyer —
Love and cats!

Maggie

ELIZABETH CAT

Written and Illustrated
by
Maggie Leonard

Maggie Leonard · Carpinteria

Cover and interior design by Maggie Leonard

Cover Art Production by
Frank Bucy, No Waves Press, Santa Barbara

Typography and graphic production by
Judy Neunuebel, Santa Barbara

Gilliland Printing, Kansas

Library of Congress Catalog Card Number 97-94300
ISBN: 0-9659853-1-8

Maggie Leonard
P.O.Box 1130
Carpinteria, California 93014

For Jim
and for Mother

I thank God, Jesus and the Holy Spirit
for the spark.

ACKNOWLEDGMENTS

The Montecito Library Saturday morning writers workshop of the wonderfuls Leonard Tourney and Shelly Lowenkopf. And group members Diane de Avalle-Arce, editing and Karin de la Pena, reading.

Debbie Murphy, Marianne Partridge, Julie Simpson, Fran Puccinelli, Mary Soto, Anne Ramsay.

Writer's Way group, Carpinteria.

FIRM EMBRACE!

CONTENTS

1

P R E T T Y   G I R L

When I first met Elizabeth it was late September and I figured she was about six weeks old and probably born in August. The exact day I didn't know, so we always celebrated her birthday the entire month of August, just to make sure.

It took Lizzy a whole year to get her look. She had started her life all in white, as though she hadn't decided at birth just how she wanted to dress. I never thought she'd be anything but a pure white cat.

But then I started to see colors and designs appear; shades of beige on her face, the middle of her back, from her wrists to her elbows and from her ankles to her backward-pointing knees. Her changing color happened gradually and I didn't notice how different she was looking until we got back from a two-week vacation. She came to meet us at the driveway and when I spotted her, I couldn't take my eyes off her.

I knew it was Lizzy but she didn't look like Lizzy. Her face had become so dark brown it almost looked black, and her fluffy, showy, skyward-pointing tail was dark brown too.

It looked like she was wearing white socks and from the back she reminded me of my high school gym teacher, who also wore white socks and was slightly bowlegged, like Lizzy.

The oil in her fur smelled something like cumin and I liked to bury my whole face in it. Long, elegant tufts of white fur coming out of the bottom of each paw decorated her small and dainty feet.

When she sat in a pincushion position and let an arm or a leg hang down, I'd tell her she had sexy legs and she would look at me with her head slightly tilted and blink dreamily.

2

We hadn't planned on Elizabeth having kittens, but when she was old enough to get spayed, it was heat season and a cat attacked her and she needed surgery on her leg. The veterinarian told me she couldn't be spayed until she recovered.

During her convalescence she got pregnant. By two different cats, as it turned out.

Star was born at eleven o'clock in the morning and we were excited to welcome this pure black little girl.

Although it seemed unusual to us for a cat to have a one-baby litter, I supposed that it was because Lizzy was petite. She weighed only seven pounds.

We went to bed that night with mother and daughter asleep in a box in the bedroom with us. I was sleeping soundly until I was awakened by a kitten commotion. Squeals and meowing and rustling were coming from the 'nursery' and finally, I got up to check and found out I had become a grandmother again!

Grey-striped Lala, who would turn out to be shy, had made an unlikely, rousing entry into the world at one o'clock in the morning.

The babies drank Lizzy's milk and enjoyed being washed and cared for by their mother. When they were older, they ate solid food. I offered them cow's milk but they refused, preferring mother's milk.

Months later, when Star and Lala were full-grown and much bigger than Elizabeth, they were still sucking her nipples and pawing her tender pink tummy with grown-up claws.

Elizabeth was becoming impatient. She gave them pleading looks and edged away. But every time she lay down, her two attachments would show up. I felt sorry for her. Nursing had obviously become uncomfortable, as well as annoying. She could never rest.

So, one day, about six months after Star and Lala were born, mother Elizabeth took a stand. She was lying down for a quiet nap when her "little darlings" arrived for eats. But this time Liz hissed and snarled at them, much to their amazement.

Oh, were they amazed. They sat up immediately, and with wide eyes, looked at mother and tiptoed away. They never drank Elizabeth's milk again.

But this wasn't the beginning of an estrangement between them. Rather it was an event that taught the girls respect for mom. Liz and Star and Lala continued to groom each other and sleep snuggled together.

3

THE KITCHEN DOOR

The kitchen door became an historical landmark as far as cat happenings were concerned. It was through this French door I saw Elizabeth present her babies with their first rodent meal. She herself never ate mice or rats or birds or lizards or even those beautiful Monarch butterflies she caught and delicately held in her mouth and brought to me.

She always brought me the butterfly gifts. Somehow she knew the other creatures she caught would not go over well with me. She would make that deep noise she always made when she had a goodie in her mouth she was delivering to someone, as if to say, "Wait til you see what I've got for you."

Star and Lala were playing on the porch steps and I was washing dishes when Elizabeth arrived making that special sound of warning or delight, depending on one's point of view, and holding a mouse in her mouth which she put down in front of them.

It was alive and the babies immediately caught on to the 'cat and mouse' game. They chased it, teased it, tossed it up in the air, and when they finally got tired of playing with it, they killed it and ate it up.

Lizzy watched with pride, yet nonchalance. I watched disgusted and mesmerized at the same time, as the last morsel was sucked up. The rigid tail disappeared slowly into Lala's mouth.

It was this same door Lizzy tried to open herself. Although I was eager to please her, I could not always predict when she would need a door opened and which door it would be.

Even in her early years she didn't meow much for door service and later on she stopped meowing at all when she wanted to go out or come in. She simply arrived at the door, sat down and waited patiently. Sometimes I would even find her tucked in a semi-circle, asleep on the doormat. I would look at her with surprise and admiration. She had the calm ability to make good use of her time while I found my way to her.

But one day, early on, Lizzy either got impatient with my faulty radar or she didn't want to bother me or maybe that well-worn brass door knob, hanging slightly askew, caught her attention.

She hung from the rattly knob, paw over paw, and slid off, one paw and then the other. It would have worked too, except this door was almost always warped from the rain. She tried over and over again, scaring me every time as the rattling echoed through the house. It took me a while to realize this cat burglar was not to be feared.

Lizzy soon got her very own door. We replaced a lower French window pane at the back of the house, with a swinging board, and she was happy to come in and out whenever she pleased. The neighborhood cats and opossums and raccoons were happy to come in, too.

And it was at the kitchen door where I first laid eyes on my Elizabeth. We had just bought the house and were doing some cleaning before moving in and although getting a cat was definitely high on my list, the last thing on my mind that day was a cat.

"Is this your cat?" I heard a young voice ask. "I found her sleeping in a pile of leaves in front of your house."

I spun around and saw a little boy standing at the open door, holding her snugly in the crook of his arm. Four feet pointing straight up in the air, long white fur all over the place, and those big, blue, loving eyes staring right back at me.

She was irresistible.

4

TOO MUCH BOTHER

When the cats were young, I thought about getting rid of them because I was busy painting the house and they were pests. I didn't want three cats. They were too much bother.

There were litter boxes to maintain and meals to serve and 'mistakes' to clean up. There was learning how to walk without tripping over cats all the time, and learning how to sleep five on the bed.

There was finding someone to feed them whenever we were away, and chasing bad cats away and offering to pay to get that one exceptionally mean tom cat neutered.

There was baby Elizabeth asleep on the lower rung and me trapped on top of the ladder. There were single-file marches to the outdoors to explain what dirt was for. And then of course, there was the assorted wild life found indoors dead or alive.

I complained to everyone about my cat problems until one day when a dear friend asked for one of the kittens for her young children.

"NO!" I snapped, embarrassed at my sharp response.

Even though she is a wonderful and caring person, I didn't think she had the time or the inclination to pamper my cats the way they were already accustomed to.

The shocking possibility of parting with them brought me to my senses.

5

No Bones About It

If I tell you cats don't have bones, you're probably going to wonder what holds their skins in the general shape of a cat. I don't know. Maybe it's starch or helium or reverse personal gravity or it could be will power or just plain habit — thousands of years of habit. But I know it can't be bones.

How many millions of times have human feet stepped — and stepped hard — on silent, vulnerable cat feet and how many cats do you know have been taken to the vet for 'broken foot'?

None. Not in a lifetime of knowing cats and treading on their feet have I ever broken a bone in a cat's foot.

Oh sure, they scream bloody murder and walk off, inconsolable, leaving a trail of piercing epithets snarled out of the side of their tightly set mouths. You are left standing there feeling sorrowful and clumsy, even though it's almost never your fault, the impression of fine, fragile bones remaining under your guilty, pitiful foot. But it's only an illusion because cats don't have bones.

You might apologize to your victim for flattening their skins, but never never for breaking bones.

Further proof of the boneless nature of cats can be seen when one of these rubber-like creatures is in a full-body stretch, toes and fingertips reaching out to the ends of being. Reality or trompe l'oeil? After a careful look, your instinct may be to find a measuring tape.

When coming upon a cat hanging by its paws from a door knob trying to open the door, one looks with admiration at its human-like ability, but what's so great about imitating a human?

It's the ability to extend beyond one's usual dimensions that is cause for a double take and you can't do it with a body full of bones.

Bonelessness may also be the reason cats seek out high and narrow places for lounging. Their fur bags drape over the sides of their perch as they look on, relaxed and superior; knowing that if occasionally they fall, no problem. The only thing squashed may be their vanity.

Think about it.

6

CAT ATTACK

Sometimes, just as I would finish my last dream in the morning and begin to wake up, I felt a great pressure on my chest and thought I was having a heart attack. The heavy feeling became stronger and stronger the closer I was to waking. My fear increased as well.

When finally I woke, another sensation was added to my symptoms; gentle tickling on my nose and mouth. Bravely, I opened my eyes and was relieved and happy to find my attacker was only Elizabeth-chicken quietly nesting on my chest.

We looked at each other nose to nose. I liked this mouse's-eye-view I had of her. I was the short one now and from this odd perspective her unusually long spray of whiskers appeared even more exaggerated, sitting on my face like a giant white spider.

She wasn't rushing me to get up and feed her although I knew she must be hungry. Her soft purring vibrated gently through her toasty body and into mine. A clear, sparkling drop formed on the edge of her mouth and fell onto my chin — like a blessing. Good morning.

We thought it a luxury to find each other again every new day.

7

My Personal Pet

Star was my personal pet. That's what I called her because she stayed as close to me as we could both manage without actually occupying the same space.

She seemed to understand my moods and what I wanted her to do. She chatted all day, always looking me straight in the eye, and since I couldn't understand a word she said, I felt free to interpret her meows as I saw fit. The words I put in her mouth were inspired by her tone of voice and the length and cadence of her meowing.

A conversation with Star one morning went like this:

"Good morning Star. What a sunny day!"

"Funny?" she meowed back.

"No, not funny, I said sunny."

Sometimes I had to scold her because she insisted on sitting much too near to me when I was working at my desk, and swished her long-haired tail back and forth over my papers. Talking to her about it made her nervous and her tail moved faster and more frantically in even wider arcs, like a hairy metronome gone berserk.

I tried to work around her for as long as I could, holding up her tail, moving a bony knee. But when I got tired of that, I would ask her to leave. She tried to make herself small but it was as impossible as trying to reduce an ocean to a pond.

When finally she had enough of my nagging, she would leave with her hurt feelings and pink pouty mouth, and find another place to sleep.

Mother always said Star liked her comfort and she was right. She slept with her head on a pillow. However, she did choose a couple of questionable locations for naps.

In the summer, I often found her outside asleep under the chaise with her bottom sticking out in the sun. I was quick to point out the error of her ways, but barely lifting her head, she would reply disdainfully, "That's how I can appreciate how cool it is under here."

Occasionally, during the day she slept, for what I thought were dangerously long periods of time, completely under the down comforter on our bed. Worried she wasn't getting enough air, I came in from time to time, and nudged her to see if she was still alive. I put a sock on top of the lump to make sure we didn't sit on her by mistake.

She knew the principles of being a cat, all right. I can't remember a single time when I picked up something to read she wasn't right there between me and my book.

8

L A L A

Lala was meticulously shy. She was quiet and kept herself in the background. So even though I missed her, I didn't worry too much that she spent most of the day away from home.

After breakfast, she'd take a slow, deliberate stroll across the back lawn and disappear through the hedge. Hunger forced her to return at various times during the day but after dinner she remained at home and was part of the trio that slept at the foot of the bed during the night.

Some days, in an effort to keep her at home, I'd dangle a piece of string in front of her on her way to the back door, and with my smallest and sweetest voice I'd beg her to play with it.

But instead of entertaining her, I scared her and she scurried away faster, glancing at the little string suspiciously. Day after day through all those years, my only reward was to watch her forlorn figure leave.

I went looking for her many times, to make sure she was all right and curious to know what was so attractive out yonder. What I found was just an ordinary lawn and bush and set of front steps. I didn't understand. I'd

call her from the street and sometimes she'd look up. Uninterested, her head would drop back behind the tall blades of grass.

Then one day when the girls were about nine years old, I saw for the first time the reason why Lala wouldn't stay at home during the day.

It was insecure and controlling Star. Lala came into the house and I started talking to her in my usual cooing mommy-to-kitty voice. We exchanged a few greetings and then, all of a sudden, Star darted out from her post at the front bedroom window, agitated, and hissed at Lala.

That was all she needed. Lala, who was just as big as Star, turned right around without a protest and went out of the house, her rough, woolly coat hanging heavier on her bones, resigned to her daytime life just outside the family circle. I couldn't believe what I saw and that I hadn't noticed it before.

About a year later, when Star disappeared, Lala came back to her house and garden. She even started sitting on my lap for the first time ever. She was sweetly shy and awkward about it, but soon she would even let me hold her in my arms.

Lala. I named her after a great aunt of mine in Mexico whom I didn't know very well, but whose name intrigued me as a child. A musical name. The name of a nice person for a nice cat.

This nice cat had green, sleepy eyes with an I-hope-I'm-not-intruding expression. She was greyish with darker stripes; the markings on her face were especially interesting and set off dramatically by a grand, white bib. Her gentle disposition belied her ability and reputation as a mouser.

Lala and Star, but especially Lala, loved to eat mice, and let's face it, rats. I could almost read her mind anticipating this delicacy in total concentration:

"Rats and mice — they taste so good!

The sloppy food in my dish can't compare with their rended hide tickling all the way down the gullet and the marrow delicacy of the fine-boned carcass. Breaking into the crunchy skull is like eating a chocolate bonbon with a soft center.

Mom never gives me anything to eat that I can really get into and work at and break and tear and struggle to get down.

And what about a little heart? You gotta have heart — and kidneys and liver. Mice are a variety of texture. And they're my only warm meal — a warm buffet of organs swimming in colorful blood-sauce.

Sometimes I leave the kidneys. Mom sweeps them
up but it doesn't bother her. A dead mouse is not a
scary mouse, is her motto. Once they're dead, in
the middle of the night, she goes back to sleep
and I keep on eating."

9

T o   T h e   B u s   S t o p

My car broke down after seventeen and a half years of faithful service, and I had to go to the bank to get a loan for a new car.

I walked down the long driveway past Elizabeth, who got up from her nap on the warm concrete. (Later, when we moved, she slept in the middle of our quiet street, thinking it was our driveway.)

Soon, Star and Lala joined us. I told them good-bye and walked down the sidewalk to the bus stop. They followed. I stopped. They stopped.

"You guys, you have to go home."

Nobody moved. I went on. I had to catch the bus. Three kitties still followed. What was I going to do?

The girls had never been to the end of our front lawn. They had plenty of room in the back and sides of the house, and they also went into the neighbor's yards. Their door to the house was in the back, there was plenty of shade there, many trees to climb and a little concrete pond with Koi that

tantalized them and drew Star in once. They weren't used to the cars and commotion on the street and they avoided it.

But now, here they were, well past their self-imposed territorial limits, out in the world. Whew! What a rush. "But we're with Mom, she'll take care of us. Where is she taking us? We've never been out here. Where is she going? What's happening?" (They asked a lot of questions.)

Usually, our walks only took us around the house. Sometimes, in the late afternoon, I would have a cup of tea on the kitchen porch, and soon the girls would gather around me and we'd talk a little and start our walk.

We would head to the back and around to the other side of the house. They would get distracted by one thing or another, but catch up again. Through the side gate and almost to the front, and my little entourage would gather closer to me as we started across the front lawn, still close to the house, but their mood definitely changed.

No longer were they carefree and playful. Now they were in that little-known part of the world and they'd better look out. They would scan around them, bellies closer to the ground.

What could happen to them here that couldn't happen in the back? Certainly the back yard held a lot of excitement and danger from the animal world, including a red fox we ran into one afternoon. But they knew about that and this was the scary unknown.

The bus was coming and we were two houses away from home. How would they ever get back? I stopped. They stopped. "Go home, babies."

Nobody moved. The bus arrived. "Please go home, you guys." Little statues. They watched me get on the bus and leave. I looked back at them. Three little kitties, all in a row, looking at me with very sad bewildered faces.

How would they ever get back?

10

Walking alongside the cats wasn't easy. They simply didn't know the meaning of the words 'beside' or parallel' or 'straight ahead' or 'no tripping' or 'you walk there and I'll walk here.'

Everything started out normally; they didn't trip me and I didn't trip them. That seemed fair to me. But then, about two steps later, the girls would begin to severely intrude on my pathway. I could make adjustments for a short distance, but then I had to stop and regroup or else we would wind up at a point far away from where I intended to go in the first place. I think if I ever followed their lead, we'd end up making a complete circle.

Why did they do that? Why did they walk right into the area my next step was going to be in? Not to step on the cat was tricky. A good sense of direction and gravity were completely in play, and to abort the next step meant I would have to sprout wings and go up.

But I didn't sprout wings and most of the time I didn't step on the buster but it was frustrating. It was one of the times I wished cats had shoulders so that I could grab them and shake them!

11

T H E R E   O N C E   W A S   A   S T R A W   H A T

Some straw hats are tastier than others. All of my straw hats were tasty to Elizabeth. The first time I found out about this peculiar appetite of hers, it was too late.

Too late for my straw hat, that is. It was gone. Only a smear of evidence was left at the bottom of the tall mover's packing box.

"Where's my straw hat?" I wondered.

"Where's my straw hat?" I said.

"What happened to my straw hat?" I yelled.

Elizabeth happened to it. Hard to believe. Even harder to digest, I bet. She seemed happy and innocent as usual and never figured out why I was so mad at her.

I can understand why she was puzzled. Everything and everybody seemed to be at her disposal. She lay wherever she wanted, she was fed at whatever time she got hungry, she sat on our laps until she had enough and left. One end of the rattan sofa was her personal scratching post, I was her playmate on call, doors were opened for her. She had a queenly attitude and this

was her realm and we were her willing subjects so what could be so wrong about eating a little straw hat?

From then on I guarded my straw hats. Beware of cat. But there were close calls. Like the time I was lying in the sun with you-know-who on my stomach and the rim of my hat dangerously near her glossy black lips. Who could resist? Nibble, nibble. Get it away from her!

Most of it was saved but she managed to leave her mark on it. A mouthful-worth of straw was gone. It's funny, I didn't really get mad at her this time. I thought it was cute and I was kind of proud of her for getting it — being so quick.

My next straw hat was very expensive and she was still around when I bought it and I did take care not to leave it where she could get at it, but there is a suspicious loose straw on the rim. . .

12

DOOR KNOBS DON'T OPEN DOORS, PEOPLE DO

Soon after we moved into our new house, we provided Elizabeth, Star and Lala with their very own twenty-four-hour independent entrance and exit. It was the kitchen window above the sink, which we opened just enough for them to fit through, and then permanently bolted in that position.

Jim put together a set-up outside the window consisting of a wood shelf attached to the house about seven feet from the ground, and a narrow stick bridging the shelf to the avocado tree, engineered to hold nothing heavier than a cat.

We were excited as we admired the device that would reduce slave duty at the doors. Now we had to train our in-and-out burgers to use it.

They wanted no part of it. Nevertheless, Jim placed the reluctant and slippery trainees on the tree. The bewildered looks on their faces told us clearly they thought we were nuts.

They snarled and complained as Jim gently coaxed them on higher along the branch to the stick and then the shelf and open window, where

I waited inside with arms outstretched, ready to grab and pull them through the opening, grateful and full of praises. They were hard to train.

But achieving our independence had its drawbacks. While Jim and I were able to hang up our doorman's uniform for the most part, there was an increase in the wildlife experience indoors and nobody had to train these busters, who ranged in size from mouse to opossum and strange cats.

They all had the same handy entrance and were punctual for their stolen meals. The strange cats didn't mind the occasional inconvenience of having to wait it out behind a bush or fence after an encounter with one of us. The culprits were sensitive to all five of us and would dash out with the slightest encouragement.

Elizabeth, however, wouldn't simply allow them to make their getaway and leave it at that. She shot out the window at escape velocity — a white blur in the wake of the thief — and hit the ground running, having bypassed the stick and tree. (Years later, after Star and Lala died, Liz didn't bother chasing anyone away anymore.)

It was harder dealing with the foolhardy opossums who managed to get down from the counter but who didn't have an understanding with gravity for getting back up.

When caught standing in the middle of the floor, they managed to waddle behind something, and were blessed with the dubious ability to pretend they really weren't there, and, moreover, we hadn't seen them!

But our substantial freedom was worth the tradeoff. . .I think.

13

P O D O

I remember the day Podo showed up. It was sunny and warm and all five of us were in the back garden. Lala was deeply involved in a leisurely bath. Star was lying in a full flying-buttress position; legs and arms extended, back arched and head tilted.

Elizabeth was farthest away, sleeping on a favorite patch of warm earth. Rapid eye movements and twitching paws revealed she was dreaming. Jim was in the shade reading a book and I was getting brown in the sun. We were all within eyeshot of each other and that was very satisfying to me.

Beyond our tall hedge is a narrow view of the Pacific, an oil platform and Santa Cruz Island some twenty-eight miles away. Occasionally a sailboat or platform boat goes by. We could hear the muted sounds of the waves and children playing on the beach.

Enter a big, white, short-haired cat. Unkempt and skinny and painfully loud and chatty.

We assessed him and he gave us a quick glance and without hesitation, walked right over to Elizabeth. They had some words and he settled in.

Meanwhile, Jim and I were having a discussion of our own about whether or not we should feed the mangy stranger. We were concerned about our cats. We didn't want to upset them or hurt their feelings.

How naive we were. We had assumed that just because we were bigger and paid the mortgage and bought the cat food, we would be making this decision of ethical and financial dimensions.

Clearly, it had already been decided by the boss, Miss Lizzy. Podo could stay. Podo, as Jim named him after his childhood stuffed elephant, ate well that day and for many months after.

We had welcomed him, although with semi-open arms, but we were glad when he was on the road again because he didn't have much to recommend him. He had no manners, lacked common sense and he wouldn't let us touch him.

While our cats never talked in the middle of the night, the free-spirit wandered around the house at all hours mouthing off and claiming and reclaiming our furniture with his putrid territorial spray.

We had expected to grow to like him, but just as it is with people, not all cats are likable.

Goodbye. So long.

14

EARS, CAT

The ear betrays the sleeping cat,
like a periscope.
A porcelain, translucent
gatherer of sound.
Approaching, I look only at the ears.
A tiny flicker is processed.

15

MADDENING CAT LOGIC

She walked up to the French door. I saw her sit down and look in. Obviously she wanted to come in. She could have come in through her window entrance, but no. For some reason she came to this door instead.

I can understand that. I can reason it out. She was walking by and saw me in the sun room and this way was quicker to get in and so she came to this door. Period. That's very easy for me to understand and if I were she, I would have done exactly the same thing. So I got up and opened the door.

End of story? Not on your life. It was time to play 'puzzle them, make them want to pull their hair out.' A little game cats throw in once in awhile (perhaps a bit too often) just to keep our blood running nicely.

The game goes like this: The buster comes to the door, I open the door. The buster remains sitting there. I plead and plead for her to come in. I get sufficiently mad and she looks at me bewildered and wondering what she did wrong. And that's the game.

But is it really a game, or is it something else? Maybe it's their quirky way of getting somewhere, or not getting somewhere, like when they are walking next to you and they walk into your path. I mean, do they just not need to get somewhere in the same way I do? Perhaps these little deviations they take come from simple, uncomplicated needs.

For instance, when they are walking beside me, or trying to walk beside me, maybe their goal is only to be very near me. And so, traditional angle or direction doesn't matter to them. Yes, that's it. Tradition goes out the window and cat logic enters silently on little cat feet and catches me unawares. They should ring a bell to announce cat logic is now in effect.

"I want to walk close to mom, and since she is going forward, and not sideways where I am, I think it makes a lot of sense that I too go forward. Her forward. And how do I get there? I have to cross over in front of her, right where she is going to be."

Very simple, straightforward (no pun intended) reasoning. And the cat is probably not even taking into account the bonus of the extra closeness resulting when a big foot crushes down on a bony paw.

Applying this very simple cat reasoning to the door thing: The cat comes to the door, and whether or not said cat initially planned to come into the house to see me or to do something else, I am now standing at the doorway with the door open and that's a good thing, the cat decides.

"Mom came to see me and that's nice. Now I don't even have to go in. I can enjoy her company right here. I don't even have to move. But she's mad at me for some reason I can't figure out."

16

MISS HOSPITALITY

Elizabeth was not known for her friendliness to strangers and people she was not used to. She pretty much stayed out of reach of folks who came by and reappeared as soon as they left.

That is why her change of habits when my mother and sister, Toni, were here on this particular visit, one stormy night, caught my attention.

It happened in the sun room, a room not very accurately named, for although it is the only sunny room in the house, it is also the only room in the house where the roof merely pretends to keep the rain out.

This is the room our house guests decided to sleep in because the TV is there and Toni likes to watch late-night shows. Mother chose the roomy rattan sofa and we brought in the fold-up bed for Toni. I hoped the threatening clouds would pass us by as usual.

Because Jim had to get up early the next day, he and I went to bed shortly after dinner and the cats joined us. Well, to be accurate, we went to bed with only two cats that night. Elizabeth had chosen to sleep in the sun room. Hmmm.

I knew that meant trouble because Toni was afraid of Elizabeth and Mother didn't appreciate a certain quality in Lizzy — Lizzy knew her own mind. Mother sees that as a negative attribute. For instance, whenever Mother petted Elizabeth too long or in the wrong place, she'd give Mother sidelong glances that clearly indicated she didn't like it and to stop now so that they both might maintain their dignity.

When Mother didn't stop, Elizabeth snarled at her. Mother would get mad and say, "I don't like Elizabeth anymore." Then I would get upset because I don't understand how anyone could not like Elizabeth and besides she had a right to stand up for herself.

So, that night I got up.

I stood at the sun room door looking at the scene; Toni was standing beside the bed looking tired and defeated. Elizabeth, who had claimed the very center of the bed, was enjoying the peaceful sleep of the innocent, and Mother, who was lying on the sofa laughing uncontrollably, was the appreciative audience of the cock-eyed drama being conveniently played out before her.

I asked what was going on. Mother pointed to Toni and said, haltingly between laughs, "She's afraid of Elizabeth!"

"How could she be afraid of Elizabeth?" I asked.

And then, looking first at Toni, who had three cats of her own, and then at Elizabeth, who didn't look at all threatening to me, I asked Toni why she was afraid of Elizabeth.

Toni told me that after she finished making the bed, Elizabeth jumped in the middle of the bed and fell asleep. She asked her over and over again to get off and finally Elizabeth threw up on the bed.

"She doesn't like me," she said, sounding a little hurt and looking perplexed at the bit of coiled fur with ears.

I told Toni it wasn't personal, Lizzy must have had a fur ball.

"No," she said, "It was just plain throw-up, she doesn't like me." I tried to tell her it was special but that didn't work either.

But Toni is a good sport and managed through the night with the shameless Elizabeth, who finally deigned to sleep at the foot of the bed. And, wouldn't you know it, the rain that never falls on drought-bound California surprised us all in the early morning, creating brand new leaks that stubbornly followed Toni wherever she moved the bed.

17

TENDER FEET

Liz and the girls didn't much like walking on grass. I guess the stiff blades irritated their paws. So, they were always careful choosing the route to wherever they were going. But sometimes there was no other way to get there (somewhere) except by crossing the lawn at some point.

That's how the cat trails came to be. Because they preferred to walk the shortest distance possible when grass was involved, they kept walking the same way over and over again, each step carefully placed, thus developing a rut in the lawn.

I discovered one such trail running parallel to the hedge from the end of the cement path to the corner of the back garden. That corner was strategic, as neighborhood cats and small dogs and whoever, got through at that point, in and out of our yard. Also, there was a nice shade plant and a bench for naps and daydreaming. This well-worn trail had been in use for a long time before I noticed it.

I looked for other trails and found another one running across the front lawn. So fussy about those sensitive tootsies.

But at the same time Lizzy wouldn't think twice about going on her annual trek across the very thick and thorny bougainvillea!

The bougainvillea was growing on a fence along part of the patio. It was an old plant, thick with wood underneath it. About once a year, this venerable vine would catch adventurous, though tender-footed, Elizabeth's eye and up she'd go, onto the fence and then on to the bougainvillea.

Standing in front of it, she looked closely at the green leaves, the delicate, fuchsia-colored flowers and the sharp thorns daring her to try it. Not only did she accept the challenge, but she made the crossing each time without a thorny encounter.

If her daughters caught sight of Elizabeth on the vine, they would play follow the leader, although they never made the attempt on their own.

There seemed to be no practical purpose for this trip except the thrill of it, the challenge and the satisfaction at the end. Hmmm. On thinking about it, that's a lot to get out of an old plant conveniently located in your own back yard.

18

S H O O T I N G   S T A R

Star was strong and could jump great distances. Sometimes I was her unwilling prop and audience.

One of her favorite performances started at the bathroom window sill. From there, after much revving up of feet and with eyes focused on her destination point, oblivious to my pleadings not to jump, she hurled herself across open space, over my head and onto a narrow area on a cluttered shelf hanging on the wall behind me.

She always accomplished this stunt without falling on me or breaking anything on the shelf, but nevertheless, I was smart enough to be scared and freeze in place whenever she decided to play leapfrog with me.

Star was a big cat, but it wasn't the possibility of her abundant weight landing on top of me that disturbed me as much as the thought of how deep and how far her sharp claws would have to dig into me in order to stop that plummeting weight.

Once on the shelf, her flight plan took her over my head again, but to the other side of me and four feet straight up to the top of the shower wall, where she sat a while, satisfied that she had impressed me.

I guess that was as good a way as any for both of us to start the day.

19

TOUGHIE

There was a certain big, black, long-haired, iron-pumping tomcat who made the rounds in our area for many years. This notorious bully was tough and mean but dumb.

He was always drenched when it rained, and his matted, downcast silhouette could be seen moving slowly across our back garden. It seemed the harder it rained the slower he moved.

And so it was he caught his death of cold. And the not obvious place he chose to spend his last days was in our living room.

Enemy camp. As each of us discovered him there, sitting smack in the middle of the sofa, coughing and hacking and sneezing as loud as a grown man, we all reacted the same way; we froze in our tracks, stunned.

It was Toughie all right, and he didn't even look at us but we took the long way around the sofa anyway, tiptoeing and whispering.

He sat in a pincushion position with eyes closed, probably dreaming of his glory days now gone. There was nothing we could do for him. We couldn't catch him to take him to the vet, so we left him alone and one day he wasn't there anymore and we never saw him again.

20

PERCHANCE TO SLEEP

On cold nights, Elizabeth slept under the covers with me. We had a routine we followed almost always without a hitch; she would jump on the edge of the bed and I, being mostly asleep, would hold up the comforter automatically, Elizabeth would walk in a ways and turn around.

It was at this point things could go wrong. Sometimes she would just stand there, at the end of the dark cave, as if forgetting why she was there to begin with, and I would have to beg her, in a screaming whisper, "Make your turn, make your turn!"

After finally snapping out of her trance she would turn around and walk up and settle in the three-inch space from the edge of the bed to my side. I would put my arm around her and she would knead my arm and shoulder, dribbling at the same time.

All this was accompanied by a healthy, resonant, vibrating purr which, when in high gear and right next to my ear, seemed endlessly magnified in the dark and peaceful night.

Trying to stay asleep, I would dislodge her claws from my nightgown from time to time as the pain level required; and although I had my arm around her, I wouldn't pet her for fear of prolonging her purr mechanism. (And did I mention her snoring? As an old lady, Elizabeth snored.)

When finally she settled her head on my shoulder to sleep, my nightgown would be dribble-drenched and pitted with claw-holes but we were both blissfully content.

I used to keep both arms around her, and when I wanted to turn onto my back, I would move ever so slowly — one arm still holding her. Later, I would turn back to my original position, taking care not to disturb her too much. She allowed me a few turns per night, if I exceeded that number she ejected from her goose down and human nest thoroughly disgusted.

Even with all *her* sleeping faults, *I* never left the bed or pushed her off.

21

E A T I N G

Eating. And sometimes not eating. It was hard to say why liver, for instance, was sometimes tops on Lizzy's list of yummy foods and then suddenly it would get a mock burial or a polite about-face. Other times Lizzy simply sat by her bowl, on a table in front of a kitchen window, which meant she was giving me another chance to please her.

Which I jumped at, calling out names of different selections and hoping for a response that would end the frustrating guessing game.

She never said a word. She left it to me to read her ever-changing mind. Now let's see. What is the opposite taste of liver? What did she love only two days ago? Perhaps a totally new selection? No. She wouldn't make it easier for me.

And if I took too long deciding on the meal, I sometimes got a sweet little bite on my ankle, followed by a couple of licks to make it better.

Sometimes Liz would join me for some people-food lunch. She was aware of my every move in the house just as I always knew her

whereabouts. So, very often, she appeared on the bed next to me where I had my lunch and watched my 'soap'.

It was my tuna sandwiches she liked best. Although she would, on occasion, eat bean burritos, omelets, chocolate-chip cookies, bacon and Milky Ways. I got in the habit of bringing a little blue-and-white plate for her favorite tuna in case she showed up. But then I found out it wasn't only the tuna sandwiches she came for.

One day, when she was outdoors, I took some tuna to her on the blue-and-white plate. She sniffed it and turned her nose away. I couldn't figure it out. It was her lunch time, it was her favorite tuna and it was her special blue-and-white plate. Where did I go wrong? What did I miss?

Jim explained to me later that although Lizzy liked the tuna all right, my little social creature was drawn by the whole package; the food, plus the fact that it came from my plate and my company.

The smallest meal I ever served Elizabeth was when she was recovering from an unknown and supposedly terminal illness. She had always been a healthy cat but all of a sudden she was listless, had a high fever and could barely walk.

Jim picked her up and we took her to the veterinarian. Jim told me later he thought that would be the last time he would be able to hold

her. Her doctor injected liquid under her skin to bring her temperature down and kept her overnight for tests and observation.

We went to visit her the next day and held her and stroked her and talked to her. She threw up some bright green liquid. It was a sad time for us and when we returned the next day, the vet told us to take her home and "make her comfortable" — that ominous phrase.

We brought her home and I put her on an afghan at the foot of our bed. She didn't want to eat or drink anything. All I could do was change her blanket every time she threw up.

But we couldn't just let her fade away. In desperation, I fed her diluted chicken broth from an eyedropper for about two days. There didn't seem to be much hope. But then this tough little cat finally stopped throwing up and managed to walk to the front bedroom, jump on my lap and then onto my desk, where she fell asleep on top of a file box in front of the window.

I kept on working and talked to her quietly and read to her from the Bible. She slept on. She woke up around lunch time and I decided to offer her some solid food.

I chopped up some cooked chicken very fine and put about a quarter of a teaspoonful on a pretty little plate and placed it in front of her. She focused hard on the dot of food, and finally decided she could handle it.

She stuck her long tongue out and slowly lapped it all up and fell asleep again. It seemed to have been just the right amount of food for her in her delicate condition.

This same meal was repeated for a few more days, increasing the mount; and then happily she got back to her regular cat food menu for many more years.

Liz screamed and yelled for Jim to feed her. He couldn't open the can fast enough to suit her. She scratched his jeans. Hurry, hurry.

But when it came to me, she knew sometimes I was a little slow and couldn't help it, but I would eventually go feed her. If I was in the house, she'd come to the doorway of the room wherever I was and sit at the threshold quietly, patiently. Her padded little feet never announced her arrival.

When I finally spotted her, I'd tell her, "Lizzy, you've got to say something so I'll know you're there." But she never did.

I introduced Lizzy to eating alfresco on a hot summer day. I saw her daydreaming under the cool shade of the olive tree, the ocean breeze fanning her fur. I thought she would enjoy her lunch out there.

And I was right. She took to it right away. Now I was serving meals outdoors regularly; and even though it wasn't as convenient for me, how could I complain since it was I who had introduced open-air service to Liz?

Instead of her highness coming in the house to inform me she was hungry, she would get up from her shady spot and walk to the open back door and sit there, looking at the house. Well, OK, I took her meal out to her.

But then one day around lunch time, I saw her walk out of the house, onto the deck a few steps, do an about-face and sit on her haunches, staring at the door, obviously waiting for lunch.

I fed her, of course.

22

UPON SEEING THE CAT EATING
FROM THE DOG'S DISH

The invitation was for
a sit-down dinner —
but it looked like a
buffet to her.

23

My brother told me about Morris, his and my sister-in-law's newly acquired cat — or cat/dog, as some people refer to him because he walks alongside his humans when they go for a Colorado country walk. Morris slept with them last night for the first time — unsuccessfully.

Poor Morris, this year-old Siamese dressed in medium-length champagne-colored fur and sporting one blue eye and one red eye, thanks to a horse's hoof, was 'booted' once again but this time to the garage because he kept jumping on and off their bed and walking all over them during the entire night. Imagine!

I asked my brother why they didn't train him.

"Oh," he said, "that would take a couple of weeks and in the meantime we wouldn't be able to get a full night's sleep."

Oh, really, I thought. I don't believe there is a two-week training program for cats, but I didn't say anything. When I suggested they train Morris I must have meant, why don't you allow yourselves some time to get used to his nighttime habits, marvelling and complaining about them in equal proportions, and, before you realize it, you'll spend a cat's lifetime trying to get a full night's sleep.

I'm going to watch closely to see how long it will take Morris The Intrepid to insinuate himself into their bedroom again. Already he has made great cat-strides; for although my brother is a life-long cat-lover, my sister-in-law is afraid of cats, but is already gathering him up in her arms and bestowing kisses and squeezes and cooing admiration upon him.

So it goes. All the signs are there, Morris. It's only a matter of time.

Footnote: One month later — Morris is in the bedroom.

24

T HE   C HAPERONES

Sometimes, Jim and I wanted to go for a quick walk down the street for a couple of blocks and back. It doesn't sound like a complicated outing but it almost always was.

And the complication was the cats. They didn't mind at all when Jim and I left by car but when they saw us leave by foot, they worked themselves into a high state of alarm and lad a lot to say about our plans.

We actually considered leaving by car for our walk, but were never able to admit defeat by the tenacious three, even if it would be for our own good.

So, in order to get any aerobic benefits from our walk, we had to be cat-free, which meant we had to sneak out of the house like a pair of defiant teenagers skipping out on their controlling parents.

But we were almost always found out and there we were, at the end of the driveway, negotiating with our now-and-then guardians. We were begging them to let us go alone and they were pleading with us to stay.

At about this time, the neighbor's ears started to prick up —
"Sounds like the Leonards are going for a walk."

Eventually, the talks broke down and Jim and I started our
walk, frustrated, and the cats were stuck with their dilemma — they didn't want
to go with us but couldn't let us leave without them.

Our not too happy nor subtle chaperones followed us down
the street without sidewalks — three aging cats darting from bush to car tire to
telephone pole, screaming out their anxious concern.

We stopped many times to check on them and I would shout
back assurances of our return and hold my breath whenever the occasional car
came down the street. They became smaller and smaller and harder to spot.

All the time Jim kept telling me they would be all right. I tried
to keep on walking but I could hear them and feel their uneasiness behind us. I
couldn't go on without stopping to look back again and again.

At one point they crossed the street to get a better view of us
and always they had to deal with other cats. Even though they were a nuisance,
they were so brave.

I wondered if they thought we were leaving them forever or
if they were worried about our welfare. Actually, I believe they didn't know what
their concern was. Whatever it was, they were only willing or able to go just so
far to insure our safety.

Elizabeth's panicked excursions took her three whole houses away. Lala likewise. Hard to believe, but Star, the homebody and scaredy-cat made it as far as the ninth house.

Were they prepared to rescue us form the danger they imagined we'd find down the street? How very dear of them, although it seemed to me they had pretty much exhausted their energy by now with none left to drag us back — dead or alive.

On our way back from our aborted walk, the cats gathered close to us, relieved and glad to be homeward bound, their ordeal already forgotten.

Obviously their heart rates had increased. Ours never got a chance.

25

What Happened To Star really should have a question mark after it because we don't know what happened to her. One day she vanished.

The posters we put up describing her and offering a reward brought us only two phone calls. One of the calls started out about Star, but soon the woman was talking about her adult and pregnant daughter who had also disappeared one day without a trace.

At first I was annoyed because the cat she had seen was not even similar to how I had described Star in the ad. But after hearing her story for a while, I realized we had a bond in having both lost someone we loved and perhaps never knowing what happened to them.

One might think her loss was greater than mine, but she never said as much, I felt she honored my loss by telling me about hers. We talked for forty-five minutes.

We don't know what happened to Star but we think a troublesome new cat in our neighborhood either injured her or scared her away or both. It is a special sadness that is hard to think about because our thoughts are open to envision every horrible possibility that can befall a cat.

Star usually stayed close to me and looked me straight in the eye with her caution-colored yellow eyes that were always round and seemingly full of concern. Star was all black but I thought if I looked closely, I'd be able to see wrinkled brows.

Everything was urgent with her. Even her tail, always pointing straight up in the air, like a bold, black exclamation mark, accentuated her statements.

I was almost never able to determine what Star's life's concerns were, minute to minute. The last image I have of her, as I left the house that day, was of a pleading and begging kitty.

And it seems her worst fears came true.

26

When Lala died, Elizabeth mourned her. She was her youngest child. Elizabeth had borne her, nursed her, spent tender moments grooming her, disciplined her. She had loved her and now she was gone and her heart ached.

In the mornings, Elizabeth would go out of the house and come back after a while, stand by the back door facing the house and cry a loud, deep, painful sound.

When Lala died, that is, when we decided to have her put to sleep because she was hopelessly ill, we wrapped her little body in an afghan and brought her home from the veterinarian.

We walked straight to the back yard. Elizabeth found us there. Jim put Lala on a bench and started digging a hole. Elizabeth sat down nearby and looked quietly at the whole situation.

Then she got up abruptly, and jumped on the bench. I opened up the afghan and Elizabeth looked at Lala closely and then went back to where she had been sitting.

I told her Lala was in heaven. She saw Jim put her in the ground and cover her with dirt.

For two weeks, every day at midmorning, Elizabeth came to the back door and cried her sadness and I came out and lay on the chaise and she lay on top of me and I'd try to comfort her and she comforted me.

27

KISSING

Whenever Elizabeth kissed me I worried she might break my nose. That's right. My nose. You see, Elizabeth didn't go in for mouth kissing. She never used her sweet patent-leather lips for kissing.

She showed her affection with her nose; an up-turned affair with seal-like fur covering the slight curve and ending abruptly at the triangle of damp, pinkish flesh.

Her nose met mine with great force and slid down one side and then the other side, and back and forth, back and forth — like a duel. Dueling noses. And with as much energy and dash as, say, Zorro himself.

Whenever we were close together, she lavished me with her powerful good kisses. She never broke my nose or even bruised it, but I instinctively examined it afterwards.

But not everybody enjoyed her kisses. Jim is allergic to cats. Elizabeth didn't know that and liked hanging around him. When she heard his truck arrive at the driveway, she raced around the house and met him as he got out of the truck. She scratched his jeans and sometimes her claws pierced through to his skin but he didn't complain.

She liked sitting on his lap and encouraged him to pet her. He did, endlessly, Afterwards, he had to brush off great clumps of fur, but only after she was out of sight.

One evening Jim and I were sitting in the sun room watching TV and Elizabeth came in and jumped on Jim's lap. She sat there for a short while and then, suddenly, she stood up, and, bracing herself with her paws on his chest, began smothering Jim with a stunning display of passionate kisses. Kisses on one side of his generous and sturdy nose, and kisses on the other side, over and over again.

At first I thought what a sweet, affectionate baby, and turned back to the movie. But after about a minute, I looked again and realized that her kisses were not stopping or even diminishing in intensity.

Jim was in a daze and sitting very still. I asked him if I should take her off him and he said no. Lizzy continued pressing her soggy nose on his.

I looked away and thought of leaving them alone — it seemed like such a private moment. Five minutes later, (honestly!), she stopped as abruptly as when she had started, jumped off and went on her way.

We sat speechless for a second and then Jim dashed to the bathroom and washed his face. When he came back, his eyes were red and swollen almost shut and he was wheezing. I asked him why he didn't stop her and he said he didn't want to hurt her feelings.

I think he probably liked it.

28

THE MOCKINGBIRD

Although I never saw Elizabeth with a bird in her mouth and she was only mildly interested in their goings and comings in our garden, the mockingbirds were usually interested in Elizabeth just because she was a cat; and, they thought, their natural enemy.

For that matter, they considered us their natural enemies as well, especially when they had young ones in a nest nearby or when the mom and dad mockingbirds were out with awkward and gangly babies teaching them the ropes. Then the mockingbirds squawked their warnings to people and beast alike and swooped and pecked anyone foolish enough to be outdoors at this time.

They sometimes pecked my innocent Lizzy between her ears making her very angry. Swoop, peck and squawk. Squawk squawk squawk. Lizzy then mocked the mockingbird. With teeth clacking and fangs showing she'd squawk squawk squawk back. If she could fly she would have chased these over-excited parents out of her garden.

And this went on year after year. So, when Lizzy was old and in the last few months of her life, and we started noticing a certain mockingbird

come to visit her when she took her afternoon nap, we were amazed.

We watched from the window. Lizzy would be sleeping on the grass at the bottom of the deck ramp. The mockingbird would arrive a little later and take his perch at the end of the railing, about four feet away from Liz, and look straight down at her.

Lizzy would open her eyes, and without moving a muscle, simply look back at him. They met like this for several minutes every afternoon for many months.

Lizzy's friend continued coming for a few days after she died.

29

H O M E C O M I N G

I had been in the hospital for ten days and the afternoon I came home, Elizabeth walked into the bedroom and jumped on the bed. I reached out to her but when she saw me a frightened look came over her face as if she'd seen a ghost and she drew away from me and left the room.

I didn't see her again until Jim and I went to bed that night. As soon as we turned off the lights, she jumped on my side of the bed by my shoulder and put both arms around my neck and started licking my hair, my ear, my neck and my face.

I was filled with emotion and tears were falling quietly as she continued her tender, loving expressions.

When she finished, her arms remained around my neck and she gave a big sigh and then snuggled her head on my shoulder and we fell asleep.

Temporada de dar gracias a Dios
por todos que nos a mandado.
Es el veinticinco de Diciembre
de mil novecientos noventa y dos.

EPILOGUE
THE DREAM

The first drawing I made of Elizabeth was the one of her sitting under the avocado tree. I drew her from memory and I finished it five months after she died. Two days later, I had this dream just before I woke up in the morning.

I was holding Elizabeth under her arms,
in front of me at eye level. She was very still and I told Jim
I thought she had just died.
Just then, she wiggled and motioned to me to
come close to her. I put my ear close to her mouth and I
heard her say, "I love you."
I whispered in her ear, "I love you."
And then she died.

Maggie Leonard was born in El Paso, Texas in 1940. She was raised in Los Angeles and has lived with her husband in Carpinteria for nineteen years.

ELIZABETH CAT
Maggie Leonard
P.O.Box 1130
Carpinteria, California 93014
FAX (805) 684-0227

Name_____

Address _____

City _____ State _____ Zip _____

Telephone (   ) _____ FAX (   ) _____

Book price: $17.95

Quantity _____

Sales tax: Please add 7.75% for books shipped to California addresses.
Shipping: $2.50 for the first book and $.50 for each additional book.
                   Book rate.
Payment: Check or money order payable to Maggie Leonard.